I0877464

HAPPY FAMILY

HAPPY FAMILY

Transform Your Time Together in 15 Minutes a Day

ALICIA MUÑOZ

sheldon PRESS

First published by Sheldon Press in 2025
An imprint of John Murray Press

1

Copyright © Alicia Muñoz 2025

The right of Alicia Muñoz to be identified as the Author of the Work has been asserted by her in accordance with the Copyright, Designs and Patents Act 1988.

All rights reserved. No part of this publication may be reproduced, stored in a retrieval system, or transmitted, in any form or by any means without the prior written permission of the publisher, nor be otherwise circulated in any form of binding or cover other than that in which it is published and without a similar condition being imposed on the subsequent purchaser.

A CIP catalogue record for this title is available from the British Library

Hardback ISBN 978 1 399 82564 1
ebook ISBN 978 1 399 82565 8

Typeset by KnowledgeWorks Global Ltd.

Printed and bound in the United States of America

John Murray Press policy is to use papers that are natural, renewable and recyclable products and made from wood grown in sustainable forests. The logging and manufacturing processes are expected to conform to the environmental regulations of the country of origin.

John Murray Press
Carmelite House
50 Victoria Embankment
London EC4Y 0DZ

Sheldon Press
Hachette Book Group
123 South Broad Street
Ste 2750
Philadelphia, PA 19109, USA

www.sheldonpress.co.uk

John Murray Press, part of Hodder & Stoughton Limited
An Hachette UK company

The authorized representative in the EEA is Hachette Ireland,
8 Castlecourt Centre, Dublin 15, D15 XTP3, Ireland (email: info@hbgi.ie)

Contents

Introduction 1
How to Use This Book 15
Family Soft Skills & Checklist 33
Family Connection & Assessment 49

PROMPTS 55

Conclusion 209
Acknowledgments 213
Your Notes 215

Dedication

To Mike, Lucas, and Luna—our newest family member—who reminds us every day that sometimes happiness is as simple as taking a walk, shaking it off, and coming home.

Introduction

When my husband and I first brought our newborn son home from the hospital, I remember feeling awe and gratitude as I stared at his quizzical, otherworldly face. The unconditional love flooding my body as I sat in an armchair and rocked him was unlike anything I'd ever experienced. *Who knows?* I thought. *This feeling could make everything easier. Maybe I'll be able to manage stressful situations better.* More than anything else, though, I hoped the feeling would last.

By the time our son arrived, I'd already read a lot of psychology books. I'd done personal growth work that included individual and couples therapy as well as family therapy sessions with my mom. I'd even learned about family systems theory and attachment research at New York University, graduated with a master's degree in counseling, and become a relationship therapist. The different frameworks I'd studied offered a way of understanding the impact families have on our wellbeing, and how we relate to ourselves and the world around us. The classes I'd taken had confirmed what I knew from personal experience: family life is complicated.

But that night, as endorphins coursed through me, a cascade of future happy moments filled my mind. I pictured my husband and me encouraging our son to take his first steps. I saw us helping him build a sandcastle. I imagined what it would feel like to jog beside him as he rode his first big-boy bike. We'd eat drippy ice-cream cones together by swimming pools on hot summer days. We'd pose for pictures in front of the Eiffel Tower, the Flatiron Building, and the Sydney Opera House. There'd be new friends and old friends, toothless smiles and visits from tooth fairies, amusement park rides in middle school, selfies on prom night.

Of course, I knew families also make us miserable. As a kid, living with my mom, dad, and older brother, I'd felt like a lone wolf trapped in a cage with other lone wolves. All of us stayed out of each other's way (unless we were eating a meal or doing something else that required us to spend time together). Looking back now, I see that we all longed to connect. But whenever we tried, hurt feelings followed. My mother would disappear into her work and friendships. My brother would shut down and go to his room. My father would seethe and eventually lash out at someone. My way of coping was to make myself as small and inconspicuous as possible while dreaming about the day I'd finally grow up and escape.

Eventually, I *did* grow up and escape my family. I chose a college in a different country, which minimized how often I returned home. The problem was, without consciously being aware of what I was doing, I carried my beliefs about family life into every new relationship I had. One of those beliefs was that the first and most important step when it comes to achieving family happiness is avoiding unhappiness in all its different forms, at all costs.

Of course, avoiding unhappiness doesn't work. Over the years, I've learned that, at best, families help us feel safe and understood—but, even then, they don't bring consistent happiness. Because children grow up and parents grow older, the power dynamics in families are always shifting. Relationships change. Aging parents become dependent on adult children, who then have the surreal experience of parenting their own parents. What families *can* do is provide us with an ecosystem that helps us develop and grow. Any vibrant ecosystem contains tensions, storms, and dry spells. Ecosystems are made up of networks of interdependent, sensitive, living organisms. Families—and ecosystems—are incubators. They supercharge growth. And the thing about growth is that it's usually uncomfortable. Even when it's necessary, it doesn't feel particularly good. Growth usually involves a whole lot of unhappy moments.

We all carry painful memories of unhappy moments we experienced growing up in our families. Unlike many of our bonds with acquaintances, friends, and work colleagues, connection with family runs deep. You sense, take in, and attune to the people in your immediate family, as they do to you. Your parents', siblings', or child's mood can be a toxin or a form of nourishment. Family relationships bring out the best and worst in us in ways other relationships don't. If our unhappy memories of family life were packed into a secret family photo album, we'd try to hide or destroy it. We wouldn't want anyone—including ourselves—reminding us of what it contained.

Over the years, I've developed a begrudging appreciation for the growth potential that lies at the heart of our unhappy moments. When we're able to meet unhappiness and discomfort with curiosity, awareness, and support, it expands our humanity. More than anything else, unhappiness is a wake-up call in relationships. It says, *Pay attention.* It asks, *Will you remain present for this and see what might need to change?* I'm not suggesting that trauma, cruelty, and neglect don't happen in families. They do. Pain can overwhelm our nervous systems when there's a great deal of unrelenting stress in a family. When this happens, it may be necessary to seek help from a trusted mental health professional. But, at the same time, *some* pain is inevitable and unavoidable, even in families experiencing moderate amounts of stress. Author and mathematical statistician Nassim Nicholas Taleb says that hardships aren't just inevitable, they're an essential ingredient in our growth. Unhappiness, losses, stress, painful events, and failures help us develop *antifragility*, a form of resilience we need—not just to survive, but to thrive. If we regularly ignore the messy, hard, unhappy, and shameful moments of family life, then we also ignore opportunities to wake up and learn. We ignore the invitation to grow.

Although unhappy moments are challenging, they're also precious, because they nudge us to create a better future. If you're holding this journal, I suspect you're someone who's open to being nudged, and willing to make small changes for a good cause. Maybe it was even an unhappy moment in your family life that led you to this book. So how do we make small changes that will influence our family's ecosystem? What small actions have the biggest impact? What interpersonal skills will help us become more connected, loving, patient, and tolerant? What actions can our six-, seven-, and eight-year-olds—and even our preteen and teenage kids—practice to enjoy family life more? And what can parents do to model the kinds of behaviors they want to see in their children more often? This journal offers answers to these and other questions, and plenty of opportunities to practice new skills.

Seven years after that first night home with our son, I left my job at Bellevue Hospital. I'd been providing group, individual, and couples therapy to New York City residents suffering from mental health issues after the 9/11 attacks. Living in our cramped apartment had become untenable, and we finally made the move to Virginia. My husband got transferred to a new position in the government organization he worked for. Our son said goodbye to his childhood friends as he entered second grade in an unfamiliar school. I opened a private therapy practice.

When people asked us, "Why would you give up city life for the suburbs?" we answered, "Fewer crowds, more trees." We were convinced there'd be more ease and less stress in a peaceful, suburban town. And we were tired of sleeping in a bedroom the size of a walk-in closet.

But, even after we moved, we found ourselves racing everywhere, just as we had in the city. We rushed to and from work, our son's school, home, soccer games, grocery stores, and routine dentist and medical appointments. Yes, there were more trees and fewer people, but my husband and I still got impatient with each other. Our son still argued with us about brushing his teeth, taking baths, getting dressed in the morning, and a hundred other everyday things. In many ways, we were just as anxious as we'd been in New York. Sometimes, it was hard to remember why we'd chosen to pour so much of ourselves and our emotional and financial resources into the unpredictable group experience known as *family life*. Where was the effortless kinship and solidarity? Where was the happiness we'd been dreaming of since before our son was born? We did still have good times together, but then something would happen that ruined the easy, relaxed vibe. The more pressure we put on ourselves to be happy, the unhappier we felt.

"I wish we'd never moved," our son said one evening at dinner, pushing macaroni and cheese back and forth across his plate. "I want to go back to our old apartment in New York."

My husband gave me his "we're in trouble" look: one eyebrow raised, lips pursed.

I felt a chill creep through my stomach. *Doesn't he remember how little space we had in our old apartment, the crowded subways, the constant noise? He's too young to see the bigger picture.* Luckily, I had enough sense to take a breath and practice reflective listening, which involves paraphrasing what you've just heard someone tell you. This is a technique many therapists use with clients to stay focused on what's just been said (you will learn more about reflective listening and how to use it with family members as you go through this journal).

"So you wish we'd never moved," I said. "It sounds like you miss our old home."

Our son started shredding a napkin. His eyes glistened.

"What did you like most about where we lived before?" I asked.

"I liked our apartment," he said, shrugging. "It was small. I always knew where you and Dad were. In this house, you don't hear me calling you if you're upstairs. It's scary."

My husband took a sip of water. "Makes sense. This house is bigger."

"I wish we could shrink it to be the size of our old apartment," our son sighed.

"That would be hard to do," I said, resisting the impulse to say something about how our son would probably complain that this house was too small when he was a teenager. "But maybe there's something Dad and I could do to help you feel less alone if we're in another room."

Our son put a fork of macaroni in his mouth and chewed, looking pensive.

"Wait, I know!" His face brightened. "What about a secret code? When I tap the wall"—he rapped his knuckles twice against the wooden table—"that means, 'Do you hear me?' Then you hit the wall to say something back." He rapped his knuckles against the table four times to demonstrate. "That means, 'Ten-four, we hear you loud and clear.'"

"I like it," my husband exclaimed, turning to me. "Do you think it could work?"

"I'm ready to test it out," I said. "We may need some training."

Our son leapt up from the table, ran upstairs, and began rapping his knuckles against the walls. We rapped our knuckles against the kitchen wall in response.

From that night on, we made a game of asking more questions at mealtimes. *Who's your favorite teacher? Why do you enjoy their class so much? If you could be any musician, who would you be and why? How would you describe a snowflake without using the words "cold" or "white"?* Following our lead, our son began asking us more questions, too. Asking the right kinds of questions is a powerful practice. Questions help people strike a balance between closeness and distance. They show that you're interested while allowing the listener to respond however they want. In and of themselves, questions communicate, "I'm curious, I care, and I want to know more about you." They offer us a way to celebrate our differences while affirming that we're on the same team. They provide a time-out from family hierarchies and level the playing field between older and younger generations. When we come to expect engaging conversations with family, it's a lot easier to shut down our smartphones and spend quality time together.

Two decades of working as a therapist has taught me that all of us have remarkably similar goals. When it comes to families, we want to be able to show up authentically. We want to be our truest selves and feel seen, accepted, and loved. But we can't do this until we set aside other tasks and relax our judgments and expectations. Within a family that's well intentioned and safe, it's easier to let down our guard. We can communicate directly rather than avoiding difficult conversations. We can set flexible boundaries and get curious about what other family members like, think, feel, and dream about. We can stop numbing our fears, anxieties, and loneliness with distractions like social media, gaming, alcohol, overeating, shopping, and overworking. We can practice new behaviors that become healthy habits until being present feels better than tuning out.

There's nothing wrong with pursuing happiness as long as it doesn't become a rigid goal, and as long as we can appreciate the value of antifragility. Embracing all our experiences within a family helps make closeness possible. Recognizing our mistakes and engaging in small, everyday practices that foster growth is what will *actually* make us happy. I've written this journal to help you and your family do that—and have a really good time together along the way

How to Use This Book

Even just 15 minutes a day of being open and curious can foster connection. But 15 minutes a day can be hard to come by. *I can't, I'm busy* may be the most repeated phrase in modern families, these days. Sitting down for a meal is challenging when everyone is doing their own thing in different rooms. When our jobs sneak into our homes in the form of emails and text notifications, it's a lot harder to focus on one another. When kids spend so much time gaming, watching YouTube videos, and scrolling through bottomless social media feeds, it's hard to come up with creative ideas together, share random jokes, tell stories, or just spontaneously hang out. Over the last few decades, our approach to family life has been transformed by technology. Spearheading ordinary activities like going for a walk or tossing a frisbee can feel like a *Survivor* episode—the parental equivalent of moving a heavy chest across an ocean floor. It's hard to wrestle family members into the here and now.

Think of this journal as a discovery portal. To enter it, to-do lists and devices must be set aside. When you pick it up, be willing to get curious about things and people you take for granted. You'll have the option of participating in activities drawn from themes introduced in the prompts. Each family member will be engaging in different skills. Many of the questions you'll be asking and answering will help you slow down and connect—with yourself and others.

Exploring a wide range of topics in a small group reveals new perspectives. If someone is shut down, the right question can pique their interest. If someone feels guarded, it can lower their defenses. Thought-provoking questions and prompts foster closeness, strengthen trust, unearth possibilities, and increase understanding. When connection becomes something to look forward to, wrangling everyone into the here and now gets easier. Sometimes, 15 minutes a day is all we need to break the trance of our chronic busyness and emerge from our silos. My hope is that, by engaging with the questions and prompts in this journal, you'll reduce the number of times you hear *I can't, I'm busy* in your own family.

LIKE, THINK, FEEL, DREAM, AND DO

This book is a choose-your-own-adventure experience. It'll provide suggested routes and guideposts, but you'll be doing things your own way and exploring uncharted territory. Read the questions and prompts anywhere you like, any time that works—during a camping trip, a long car ride, at a meal, over tea or coffee, in a waiting room, at a holiday event or a birthday party. Read one, two, or three prompts at a time. Read and respond to four today and only one tomorrow. Commit to answering the same question or prompt in one sitting, or answer different ones at the same time. Mix and match. Decide together what everyone wants to do, and do it.

Beneath each prompt, there's space for your written responses. Use it to jot down words or phrases that will help you make note of, and remember, what you and others share. If you need extra space, you'll find blank pages for jotting notes at the back of the book.

The prompts fall into four categories: *liking*, *thinking*, *feeling*, and *dreaming*. There's also a fifth category: *doing*. The first four prompt categories are accompanied by a symbol to help you recognize each at a glance:

liking

thinking

feeling

dreaming

The doing prompts appear in a series of boxes at relevant points in the journal. Inside each box, you'll find a mini adventure meant to help you translate what you've been learning into concrete behaviors.

Some family members will prefer one category over another. Identifying prompts by their symbol helps you select the prompt category quickly and easily. For example, prompts in the feeling category can make some family members uncomfortable. They may need to hear other people answer before they do. Listening to what others say will influence every family member, and spur reflections related to each category. You may find thinking prompts don't make sense to family members who are less cerebral or introverted, and that they prefer responding to dreaming prompts or engaging in doing prompts. Whatever the people in your family prefer is fine! There are no better or worse prompt categories, and no right ways to respond. Because the prompts and activities you'll be exploring here aren't attached to a calendar, you don't have to answer or do them in order or within a preset time frame. Engage with them in whatever way suits your needs best.

Here's a breakdown of each category, along with its focus and purpose:

Liking prompts

What you like is a big part of who you are. Recognizing your own and others' likes fosters understanding. It supports a more reciprocal relationship between you and others. When you know what someone else likes, it makes it easier for you to take their preferences into account when you make decisions. Without reciprocity, family members feel ignored and bulldozed, and you'll hear "It's not fair!" a lot more often.

It's important for parents to understand and validate their children's preferences, even if they don't always accommodate them. It's also important for children to get a peek behind the curtain of their parents' preferences. Understanding fosters trust. When your kids trust you, they'll share more with you. When you trust them, they feel it, and are more invested in being trustworthy. The more we get what our kids are feeling and experiencing, the more we're able to support them through challenges—even if the support they need from us is to let them figure things out on their own.

When we don't agree with what others in our family like, it's tempting to judge them or even try to change their minds. But nonjudgmental acceptance of others' likes is an essential practice in families where we're trying to model empathy and tolerance.

The liking prompts will help you get to know each other better and appreciate the things that make each family member unique. This deactivates judgments, tensions, and power struggles. Instead of wasting time and energy trying to convince people to like what you like, you'll let people be who they are more often. You'll increase your capacity for others' distinctive tastes, styles, and ways of enjoying themselves. You'll come to respect others' freedom to choose differently than you would, and you may even discover surprising areas of overlap between your preferences.

Thinking prompts

Distinguishing between helpful and unhelpful mental patterns in the presence of nonjudgmental family members requires safety and trust. It's a way of cultivating a particular kind of mindful presence together. These prompts encourage everyone to view thoughts as intangible "things" we *have* rather than the core of who we *are*. They invite reflection on how thinking is a tool to help us plan and organize, make meaning, and predict the future. If we act on our thoughts blindly, without vetting them for accuracy, they have the potential to cause us and others harm.

Thinking prompts help kids develop metacognition skills—the ability to observe their mental processes and think about the way they think. Learning specialist Marc Gladstone reminds us that by encouraging children to develop metacognitive skills early on we can help them to become independent learners and strengthen their self-advocacy skills (i.e. their ability to speak up for themselves). These prompts remind parents that they, too, may want to practice engaging in self-reflection more often, hone their problem-solving skills, receive feedback gracefully, and learn from their mistakes. In families, we're all works in progress, and we all benefit when we're able to step back and observe our judgmental, reactive thoughts rather than assuming that we have a monopoly on the truth, making hurtful accusations, or lashing out.

By shining a spotlight on unconscious processes such as self-criticism and defensiveness, thinking prompts promote self-awareness. They help family members identify, consider, and assimilate diverging viewpoints. Thoughtfulness is an evolving capacity in younger children, preteens, and teenagers—one that adults model when they pause, get curious, listen, and become more thoughtful themselves.

Feeling prompts

The better we are at sensing our own emotions without being swept away by them, the better we become at sensing others' emotions, too. This helps us relate to others on a deeper level and pick up on the nuances of interpersonal situations more accurately. Feeling literacy is a skill that takes time and practice to develop and hone. Knowing what you yourself feel isn't as easy or simple as it sounds—it's more of an ongoing practice than a one-and-done event. Not only does it increase feeling literacy, but it's also a way of self-soothing. Just sensing and labeling feelings accurately can reduce overwhelm. From a less emotionally reactive place, we make wiser choices.

For example, if a person identifies the tension in their throat as anxiety, they're able to take a mental step back from the way they're perceiving a situation. They can ask themselves, "Is there anything to worry about in this moment, right now?" They have a chance to pause and tune into their body, label what they feel, distinguish what they feel from reality, and notice their anxious thoughts. When kids practice noticing their feelings instead of indulging their impulses, they're better able to self-soothe. They have access to a range of internal emotions without having to deny, repress, or avoid them.

Everyone needs practice and support feeling what's hard to feel. Hearing how others in our families experience and handle anger and work through sadness normalizes these challenging emotions. We learn we're not alone in our struggles with self-criticism and shame, and, together, we can begin to crowdsource strategies for coping with stress.

Dreaming prompts

Dreams give us a space where we have freedom to simply be. As helpful as it is to organize family life around ordinary, necessary, and predictable events (waking up, going to bed, sharing meals, working, going to school), we also need unstructured dream time. Kids are usually good at dreaming, but adults sometimes need help remembering to dream. Tricia Hersey, founder of The Nap Ministry, believes cultivating time and space to dream isn't a frivolous pastime. She sees it as revolutionary—an antidote to grind culture.

Dreaming prompts help us transcend challenges and problems. They help us refuel. They're designed to support everyone's dreams in a family, no matter how big or small, and to encourage us to tap into creativity. They invite us to enjoy being alive by going on adventures and trying new things. When we dream big, life is richer.

Doing prompts

Doing prompts remind us to act on what we've discovered and learned. They convert themes, ideas, and responses gleaned from the other prompt categories into creative experiments and mini adventures.

Whether you revamp an old game, engage in a weekly challenge, or create a gratitude touchpoint, doing prompts can be adapted to suit your family's preferences and schedule. Most can be completed in around 15 minutes. When you do them is up to you. Maybe you wait till everyone's in the mood, or maybe you do them each time you reach a doing prompt box, no matter what! (Note: some doing prompts will require common household items you likely already have, such as kitchen utensils, paper, pens, and tape.)

SETTING YOURSELF UP FOR SUCCESS

Here are a few tips to inspire cooperation as you proceed through this journal, along with some suggested ground rules for creating positive family experiences:

Share your "why"

To inspire others to participate in a family journal practice, begin by sharing what's motivating you in a way that's genuine and vulnerable. Connecting with your "why" is a way of setting an intention—an overarching goal that reflects your values and hopes. Intentions can be powerful navigational tools in a family, because each time you remember them, they reorient you in ways that help you stay on track. Is your intention to become a more patient, understanding, or curious person? To connect more with a partner, kid, sibling, or parent? To enjoy the ordinary, everyday moments of life and have more fun? To slow down and be less task-focused? Will understanding others better help reduce conflicts and misunderstandings?

Connect with your "why" and share your intention regularly.

Ask your family what they want

Find out what others might like to get out of a family journal practice. Would they enjoy more spontaneous, quality time together? Do they want to feel more relaxed and at ease? Would they like to share more about themselves without feeling as though being honest triggers a parent's or partner's anxieties or judgments? Do they want to laugh more?

Invite collaboration from the get-go

Allow family members to weigh in on when and where you'll read prompts and engage in activities. The last thing you want to do is turn something meant to be fun into a chore or an obligation. Listen to everyone's ideas. Does anyone have suggestions on how to turn the prompts into a daily or weekly ritual, game, or challenge? Could you offer a small prize for consistent participation?

Agree on the number of prompts you'll respond to

Make a commitment to respond to a certain number of prompts a day (or week). This creates accountability and helps establish a ritual. Once you've created a ritual out of responding to prompts, you've already transformed new behaviors into a healthy habit. Will everyone commit to a question a night on the days you're at home together? If not, what can family members commit to?

Decide on optimal times

When does everyone in your family find themselves together in the same space? At breakfast? Dinner? Driving somewhere in the morning or at night? Lounging around on the living room couch in the evening? Convening in the kitchen before bed? Decide on the best times to read journal prompts. If everyone's busy, brainstorm ways to adjust your schedules to create 15 minutes of regular family time every day—or every few days.

Pair this journal with another pleasurable activity

Pair reading prompts with other activities you already enjoy or do together on a regular basis. Do you sit down at a table or counter for an afternoon snack? Do you eat dessert together after dinner? Do you take walks on weekends or go on hikes? Do you commute together on buses, trains, or subways, or listen to music together in a car? Try engaging with this journal when you're already having fun doing something else, and feeling relaxed, open, and receptive.

Don't take it personally when others are less motivated than you are

When you suggest creating a family journal practice, kids or partners may roll their eyes and say, "That's corny" or—as I've already mentioned—"I can't, I'm busy." Respect that! Reread this list of tips. Pinpoint where you need to circle back and enlist your family's cooperation. Do you need to experiment with fresh, creative ways of getting others' buy-in? To communicate your "why," and the benefits to those in your family? Do you need to put together a realistic list of times when others are available? Do you need to rearrange your own schedule?

Timing is everything

Finding moments when everyone is open and willing to engage in a new practice is a matter of timing. If your kids are looking forward to meeting a friend, going somewhere, or playing a game, family connection will take a back seat for the time being. But that doesn't mean it can't be a priority tomorrow.

Put away devices

In his book *Stolen Focus: Why You Can't Pay Attention*, Johan Hari highlights how our cell phone, which is always within reach—in our pocket or in our bag—leads us to do the easy thing, rather than the important thing. As you proceed through this journal, give yourselves a fighting chance of doing the important thing: spending quality time together.

Make sure everyone has put away devices before you begin reading or answering prompts. Consider setting screen-time limits with family members. Agree on device-free zones in cars, bedrooms, dining rooms, bathrooms, and kitchens. You may even want to institute a centrally located "device parking lot" in your house—a designated bowl or box by the front door or in a closet where devices are placed and forgotten about for a preestablished time period.

Family Soft Skills

As you go through this journal, you and your family will practice and strengthen a variety of valuable interpersonal skills, which I've called *family soft skills.* These are ways of being and behaving that make interacting safer and more fun because they help everyone lower their defenses, relax, and express themselves more spontaneously and honestly.

When there's a commitment to practicing and modeling family soft skills, you're also learning what engagement looks like in communities outside of your family. Business magnate Henry Ford famously said, "Whether you think you can, or you think you can't—you're right." The same principle applies to our relationships with others. When we think others will live up to our vision of them, we're usually right. Recognizing others' goodness is a form of self-interest, as is practicing a range of skills that help us relate compassionately and nonjudgmentally.

Soft skills include the ability to communicate, collaborate, show care and respect, understand your own inner experiences, listen to others, and resolve conflicts. The Family Soft Skills Checklist at the end of this section breaks these skills into steps. Read through the checklist regularly to identify where you're strong and where you need to focus your efforts. Remember: skills like these are cumulative and take time to develop—for most of us, a lifetime! Go easy on yourself when you struggle to do them or fall short.

1 TUNING INTO YOUR BODY

Take time regularly to notice sensations in your body. A pleasant warmth in your belly could be a signal that you're feeling happy or grateful. Pressure in your head or neck might be an indication that you're growing anxious. This skill—known as *interoception*—refers to our ability to be aware of our sensations and internal experiences. Practice getting to know your baseline—the whole-bodied experience you sense when you're relaxed and at ease. Notice how this experience shifts and changes throughout the day. Your body will often provide you with information that can help you take better care of it. Allow what you sense within your body to inform small choices you make, such as whether you drink or eat, stand or sit, or take a break from a task.

Notice what it's like to live in a body from one moment to the next. This may seem simple, but most of us spend a lot of time thinking about the past or imagining what will happen in the future. Being present, in our bodies, in the here and now, is an essential part of engaging in meaningful interactions with family members. If you're speaking and you feel jittery, let your family members know: "I feel uncomfortable right now. Can someone else answer this prompt?" Sharing what you notice taking place within your body can be an important part of communicating openly and honestly.

Keep in mind that some people are more naturally inclined toward interoceptive awareness than others. As you practice this skill, you'll get better at staying connected to your body while listening to and interacting with others.

2 BEING OPEN AND RECEPTIVE

A large part of what others take away from what we say hinges on *how* we say things, or the intentions underlying our words. Allow others to experience your openness and receptivity whenever you share your thoughts and opinions. Set an intention for yourself, such as "I want to enlarge the conversation when I speak, not shut it down" or "I want the people around me to know their views matter." You can also practice being open and receptive by uncrossing your arms and legs, leaning toward others, making eye contact now and then, and allowing your voice to express warmth and tenderness.

3 LISTENING

Presence and curiosity are preconditions to attentive listening. Presence is the experience of setting aside your own thoughts, judgments, assumptions, mental stories, and predictions about the future. Presence brings you into direct contact with the here and now. Your energy, thoughts, feelings, and reactions shape family interactions, even when you're not talking. Remaining interested and engaged when someone asks a question, or when someone responds to a prompt, is part of the listening process. It means containing your own impulses so another person is able to respond at their own pace, without being interrupted or feeling pressured.

Anyone who wants to practice listening can instantly enhance their communication skills with a technique called *reflective listening.* Start by focusing on the person speaking. Then, paraphrase or summarize what you've heard. Setting aside our own internal dialogue for an extended period of time as we focus our attention on another person can be challenging—test it out! If a family member responds to a prompt with "Bubble gum used to be my favorite candy when I was a kid," don't respond, "Mine, too!" Instead, reflect back what they said—not what you started to think about in response to what they said. "So I'm hearing that bubble gum used to be your favorite candy as a kid—is that right?" would be the way you might respond using the reflective listening technique. This is a technique you'll probably be using sparingly, to help those around you feel heard at key moments. Like salt, a little reflective listening enhances the flavor of conversations, while too much dulls the senses.

4 SHARING YOURSELF

For many of us, when others ask us questions, it's easier to hold back or say what's expected rather than what's true. We need to tune into our comfort level when we share, but we also need to take risks. As you practice this skill, listen to the prompt, think about it, and then sense what's true for you. Risk being honest. Use your imagination. Speak your mind. Reveal something new and see what happens. Being vulnerable isn't easy, but if you're never vulnerable, you make it hard for people around you to relate to your experience. And remember that talking a lot isn't the same thing as sharing honestly and being vulnerable. If you tend to overshare, practice sharing only what's truly important right now so others can take in what's meaningful to you.

5 SHOWING CONSIDERATION

Be thoughtful in how you select a prompt, and playful in how you read them. Ask different family members which category they're interested in responding to. Being considerate means that, if necessary, you rephrase prompts in ways that help the person you're talking to understand them better.

Even within a single family, there are differences between how intensely people feel, and the ways people think and behave. Some are more sensitive to perceived threats. Others are more cognitively inclined. Being considerate means understanding that others' brains and nervous systems are different from yours. Consideration includes a willingness to acknowledge, respect, and learn about these differences.

6 ENCOURAGING OTHERS

At the core of "encouragement" is the French word *cœur*—heart—and heart is central, too, in how we support others. When you encourage another person, you lend them your wholeheartedness to give them a boost as they move toward a goal, desire, or dream. Give family members verbal encouragement, or encourage them with your warmth and presence. Encouraging phrases include "I love learning this about you," "I never would have guessed that," and "Can you say more about that?" Encouragement means keeping the things you appreciate about family members in mind even when they're in a bad mood, or don't want to answer a question or participate in an activity.

7 RESOLVING CONFLICT

Even if you sidestep conflict by ignoring your feelings, or trying to swallow your anger and frustration, these strategies come with their own set of problems. They can lead to passive aggression, resentment, and emotional withdrawal. Rather than avoiding conflict, practice remaining connected to yourself and others at tense moments. When disagreements arise between you and other family members over the course of going through this journal, it's an opportunity to practice conflict resolution skills.

When we get into an argument with family members, it's even more important to pay attention to our bodies. Like a fuel indicator, our bodies will tell us when we're running on empty. Stay tuned in to cues like shortness of breath, a thumping heart, racing thoughts, building physical tension, general numbness, or a sense that your body is collapsing in on itself. Then, say, "Let's take a break from this discussion and come back to it in 20 minutes." Later, revisit what happened. Remain open and receptive. Share honestly and vulnerably. Was someone anxious or scared? Were feelings hurt? Be willing to see your part in the conflict. Ask "How have I hurt you?" with openness and receptivity, be genuinely curious to hear others' response, and use active listening to take in what others say. Practice apologizing, even when it's hard and uncomfortable to admit that you make mistakes. Practice receiving apologies graciously rather than leveraging them to get the upper hand over a person who trusts you enough to show humility.

FAMILY SOFT SKILLS CHECKLIST

1 Tuning into my body

- [ ] I practice tuning into my own body, and noticing my nonverbal communication.
- [ ] I notice sensations in my stomach, chest, throat, head, arms, and legs.
- [ ] I'm aware of immediate sounds, tastes, smells, textures, and visual elements.
- [ ] I balance awareness of my body with awareness of those around me.
- [ ] I practice letting what I sense through my body inform how I interact.
- [ ] I'm willing to share what my body is signaling to me with others.

2 Being open and receptive

- [ ] I practice soothing myself so that I exude a calm, accepting vibe.
- [ ] I model the kind of openness and receptivity I want from others.

- [ ] My body is relaxed, my arms and legs are uncrossed, and I make some eye contact.
- [ ] I lean a bit toward other people, and keep what I like about them in mind.
- [ ] My throat is relaxed, and my voice conveys the underlying gratitude I feel toward others.
- [ ] I see when I have judgmental, controlling, worried, doubting, or self-pitying thoughts.

3 Listening

- [ ] I give others time to respond without interrupting, pressuring, or chiding them.
- [ ] I direct my full attention onto others when they're sharing something.
- [ ] I set aside judgments, assumptions, mental stories, and predictions about the future.
- [ ] I remain interested when someone reads a prompt or asks a question.
- [ ] I remain engaged when someone responds or shares.
- [ ] I use reflective listening when needed, paraphrasing or summarizing what I've heard.

4 Sharing myself

- [ ] I notice when I'm guarded and experiment with lowering my guard.
- [ ] I tune into and remain aware of my own comfort level when I share things.
- [ ] I notice if I overshare, and experiment with containing myself and sharing what's key.
- [ ] I'm willing to risk being vulnerable in the service of connection.
- [ ] I'm willing to risk being honest and assertive while still being respectful.
- [ ] I draw on my imagination, sense of humor, and creativity to express myself.

5 Showing consideration

- [ ] I collaborate with others and share responsibilities because we're a team.
- [ ] I consider others' feelings, needs, and preferences in my choices and decisions.
- [ ] I allow myself to be lighthearted, earnest, and warm when I speak or respond.

- [ ] I rephrase, and adapt prompts for family members when necessary.
- [ ] I accept that everyone has different sensitivities to perceived threat.
- [ ] I accept that family members have different brains, nervous systems, gifts, and abilities.

6 Encouraging others

- [ ] I give others verbal encouragement when I'm with them.
- [ ] I welcome others participating, sharing, and showing up as they are.
- [ ] My vocal tone, facial expressions, and gestures demonstrate the delight I take in others.
- [ ] I nurture a genuine desire to see family members thrive and feel good about themselves.
- [ ] I use supportive phrases like "I love that!" and "I'm interested—can you say more?"
- [ ] I accept when others get irritable, without trying to save them or "fix" the situation

7 Resolving conflict

- [ ] I use soft skills to help me work through disagreements.
- [ ] I pay attention to my body, self-soothe, remain open to others, share, and listen.
- [ ] I practice being considerate, seeking to understand and accept how others are different.
- [ ] If a conflict escalates, I request a break, so everyone has time and space to calm down.
- [ ] Later, I revisit what happened with a willingness to see my part in it and learn something about myself and others.
- [ ] I ask, "How have I hurt you?" and practice apologizing and receiving apologies humbly.

Family Connection

The desire to connect is hardwired into us. Even in the womb, we're having our first experience of deep connection with another human being who provides us with safety and nurturance. When we're born, we continue seeking closeness, gravitating toward warmth and containment in the arms of caretakers. This search for safety and connection continues for the rest of our lives. Although psychologist Abraham Maslow placed the need for love and belonging near the top of his hierarchy of needs (meaning he saw it as less essential than the need for food, water, and safety), it's what enables all our basic needs to be met, particularly when we're young. It's hard to stay safe and nourished for an extended period of time without connecting to other people.

When you take the Family Connection Assessment at the end of this section, think of your bond with family members as a broad, all-inclusive, invisible umbrella that stretches across space and time. It's something that encompasses different facets of connection. It's the moments when you feel bonded or close to them, but it's also the times when your relationship changes and you feel less close. It's brief and time-limited, but it's also deep and long-lasting. It's strong and—sometimes—fragile. As you read through each statement and select your response, think of your bond as a web of tendrils between you and family members that stretches and shrinks. Though these tendrils are powerful, they're still flexible enough to remain unbroken through periods of loneliness and conflict, or when physical or emotional distance places a barrier between you.

The purpose of this assessment is to help you collect information about how you experience family connection. Take it before you begin the journal for a baseline score. Then, take it again halfway through for a midway score. Once you've completed the journal, retake it for a closing score.

If you take the assessment several times as you engage in this family journal practice, it will give you different sets of data. This will help you track how your connection with other family members may be changing and evolving due to the family soft skills you're learning and using. If everyone is open to it, you can discuss your assessments as a family and hear everyone's views. In what ways are your perceptions of connection similar or different in the five areas assessed? Are scores consistent across family members' assessments? Is connection high in some areas and low in others? These scores aren't diagnostic; they're meant to bolster your motivation as you track your own and your family's strengths and growth areas.

Take the assessment by writing your responses to each statement on a separate sheet of paper. Name and date them so they're easy to identify later. Once everyone has completed their first baseline assessment, keep them someplace where they'll be easy to find again in the future. You might want to take photos of them and store them in a digital photo album for safekeeping.

FAMILY CONNECTION ASSESSMENT

Choose the number that corresponds best with each statement.

Connection statement	Frequency 1 Never	2 Seldom	3 Sometimes	4 Often	5 Always
1 I share what I like with family members.	1	2	3	4	5
2 My family members accept what I like.	1	2	3	4	5
3 My family members share what they like.	1	2	3	4	5
4 I accept what my family members like.	1	2	3	4	5
5 There are things we all enjoy together.	1	2	3	4	5
6 I notice how my thoughts affect me.	1	2	3	4	5
7 I notice how my thoughts affect others.	1	2	3	4	5
8 I share my thoughts with my family.	1	2	3	4	5
9 My family is curious about my thoughts.	1	2	3	4	5

FAMILY CONNECTION

Connection statement	Frequency				
	1 Never	2 Seldom	3 Some-times	4 Often	5 Always
10 We have conversations about our different views.	1	2	3	4	5
11 Usually, I know what I'm feeling.	1	2	3	4	5
12 I share what I feel with my family.	1	2	3	4	5
13 I'm curious about things I do to avoid what I feel.	1	2	3	4	5
14 I pay attention to how my family feels.	1	2	3	4	5
15 We handle anger well as a family.	1	2	3	4	5
16 I share my dreams and goals with my family.	1	2	3	4	5
17 My family asks about my dreams and goals.	1	2	3	4	5
18 My family shares their dreams and goals with me.	1	2	3	4	5

Connection statement	Frequency 1 Never	2 Seldom	3 Sometimes	4 Often	5 Always
19 I care about my family's dreams and goals.	1	2	3	4	5
20 We live our dreams and celebrate goals.	1	2	3	4	5
21 I like doing things with my family.	1	2	3	4	5
22 My family likes it when I do things with them.	1	2	3	4	5
23 We all participate fully when we do things together.	1	2	3	4	5
24 We do things that involve high-energy fun.	1	2	3	4	5
25 Going on new adventures is a priority for us.	1	2	3	4	5

Scoring: To calculate your family connection score related to *liking*, add up your selections for 1–5. Related to *thinking*, add up your selections for 6–10. Related to *feeling*, add up your selections for 11–15. Related to *dreaming*, add up your selections for 16–20. Related to *doing*, add up your selections for 21–25. A score between 25 and 58 suggests lower connection, between 59 and 91 suggests moderate connection, and between 92 and 125 suggests higher connection.

PROMPTS

What nickname would you choose for yourself and why?

Explain which of the five primary tastes—salty, sweet, sour, bitter, or savory—matches your outlook on life best.

What repetitive sound or movement (rain, rocking, tapping) helps you relax?

If you ever owned a boat, what would you call it and where would you sail it?

Family fleet

Make paper sailboats and write your favorite boat name on the prow of your creations. Fill a large sink or tub with water, and set sail. Talk through your imaginary experiences on the high seas. The owner of the sailboat that sinks last gets crowned Family Fleet Captain.

What's your best memory of a family member you wish we saw more?

Tell us how you think you got your name, and what your name means (if you don't know, make it up).

Which of these six basic feelings—joy, pride, surprise, disgust, sadness, or anger—do you like having most and why?

What's a new dessert we could create now in ten minutes with everyday ingredients?

Feeling charades

Decide who will be miming a feeling, then set a timer for one minute. The person miming the feeling uses facial expressions and hand gestures. Each family member gets one try at naming the feeling being enacted. When someone names it correctly, it's their turn to mime. Once you've run out of feelings to mime, vote on who expressed which feelings best.

Why would (or wouldn't) it be better if we asked permission before hugging you?

What's one goal we all share as a family?

When someone you like disagrees with you, does it change how much you like them?

What's the name of a brand-new drink flavor—such as "fizzypopalicious"—that you could invent. Use hand gestures, sounds, and facial expressions to show us what it tastes like.

Mini-surprise party

Spend 15 minutes planning a surprise for one of your family members. Include their preferred form of entertainment. If they like clowns, figure out which family member will dress up as a clown. If they like face painting, decide who will paint faces. Then give your family member their mini-surprise party. Afterward, debrief with them about what they enjoyed.

If you could teach one subject in school, what would you teach and why?

Would it be creepier to live in a world where everyone was different but looked the same, or where everyone was the same but looked different?

Name a scary thing you've done in front of a group of people. What scared you about that?

If you could invite any three people to dinner tonight, who would you pick and why?

Frankenstein candy competition

Begin by gathering together a variety of different junk foods. Agree on the amount of time (e.g. one or two minutes) participants will have to piece together their Frankenstein candy out of the foods provided. Set a timer and begin. Once the timer goes off, line up the combos. Taste everyone's creation and vote on who made the grossest one. The participant who wins gets to decide which Frankenstein candy they'd like to eat.

Describe a moment when winning a game was so exciting you wished it lasted longer.

Sum up your life story to date in a few sentences.

What did someone say to you recently that boosted your confidence?

You're given the choice of remembering yourself going skydiving, or having no memory but only a picture proving you did it that would impress your friends. Which would you choose and why?

Name three junk foods that taste good alone but would taste gross combined.

When was the last time you laughed hard, and what was the best part of that?

When others argue, is your impulse to withdraw, join in the argument, or make peace?

How do you feel when others give you advice you didn't ask for? Give an example.

What talent could get you into *Guinness World Records*?

What's your favorite odd smell (e.g. burnt toast, dust, dog breath), and what do you like about it?

Which famous villain do you admire and why?

How does loneliness feel different than sadness?

Which talents could get each member of our family into *Guinness World Records*?

Family world records

Family members take turns competing to be the reigning family champion in their talent area, whether it's making animal sounds, juggling tennis balls, standing on one foot for five minutes straight, or reciting Pi.

If you could have three musicians performing on the same song, who would they be and what would they sing about?

Which social skill is easy for you (making small talk, listening, being patient, comforting people, cooperating, taking turns, showing empathy), and which one do you find hard?

When you've hurt someone's feelings, what do *you* feel?

What's a small thing we could do to create less waste or save energy?

The name game

For 15 minutes, you'll be trading names with someone else in your family. Decide on whose name you'll be called, and who'll take your name. Once everyone has settled on the name they'll be assuming, grab a ball and toss it back and forth between you. Whoever has the ball calls out their family member's "temporary" name and throws them the ball. Take on the mannerisms and personality of the person whose name you've temporarily assumed. Avoid throwing the ball to the "wrong" person. When you're done, debrief on the experience of assuming another family member's name.

Describe your first memory in detail.

How does it feel when someone who hurt you says they're sorry and really means it?

Sing your favorite song for 30 seconds with your tongue between your teeth until we guess it.

What's one good thing you had too much of, and how did you know you'd had too much?

If you could stop worrying about the one thing you worry about most, what problem in your life might begin to change?

If you could create a protective magic circle of people or creatures to think about when you felt scared, who would they be?

Who do you look up to, and what do you admire about them?

Magic circle

Everyone draw a circle on a piece of paper with their name in the middle. Write the names of the people (or creatures) you'd position around you in difficult moments. Favorite protective people might be family members, others might be friends, still others might be imaginary or fictional beings. Draw images rather than writing names, or create a magazine clipping or photo collage. Keep your magic circles where you see them regularly.

If you could eat a color, which one looks yummiest, and what would it taste like?

When did you do nothing instead of distracting yourself, and what was that like?

When something scares you, are there words or phrases that calm you down?

What's a new machine you could invent? What problem would it solve?

Do nothing together

Create a list of your favorite examples of doing nothing as a family. Is it when you sit around a room engaged in different "mindless" activities? Is it when everyone is milling around the kitchen on a Sunday morning? Is it after breakfast but before family members have begun going about their day? Is it when you're driving somewhere? Place this list where everyone in your home will see it daily. As you go about your week, whenever you notice yourselves doing nothing together, share what you enjoy about "do nothing" time.

Choreograph a one-minute dance to your favorite song with us as the dancers.

Describe the closest you've come to experiencing déjà-vu—a feeling of having already been in this moment right now before.

When you feel sad, what do you do to feel less sad?

What's a new, fun way we could play an old game we used to enjoy?

What are three logical reasons why a rule you find dumb might be necessary?

Do you relax more when your day is planned or when it's unplanned?

What do you have so much fun doing that you'd like to do it as a full-time job?

____

____

____

____

____

A new twist on an old game

What adjustments would add an element of surprise to a familiar, beloved game? Decide on the game or games you're going to modify. For a board game, up the ante by setting a time limit on each person's move or turn. Increase the consequences of making a wrong move, or create a reward (such as prize money, or an extra move for landing on a particular space). For an outdoor game, increase the difficulty by limiting your mobility (e.g. securing one arm to your body; wearing a mitten). Play the game with your adjustments. If it's more fun with the adjustment, keep playing it this way!

Describe the best beginning of a favorite book and why you like it.

What's the main difference between how kids and adults act toward their friends?

When was the last time you shared good feelings with another person who felt happy on your behalf?

Describe the weirdest alien from another planet. What would it do that you can't?

What do you like most about being you?

What's a family motto that fits us (e.g. *Perfectly imperfect* or *There through thick and thin*)?

Identify three things you're grateful for. What's it like to share them with us now?

What's a goal you want to achieve, and how would your life change when you achieve it?

Family motto

Gather your ideas for a family motto, write them on slips of paper, and fold these slips into squares. Then, close your eyes, select a square, unfold it, and read the motto it contains. Make a minute-long argument about why you think this motto fits your family best (regardless of whether it's your slip of paper or someone else's). Once everyone has argued for the motto they selected, vote for the best one. If more than one motto fits, use both. Finally, decide where you'll place this motto—such as on a coffee mug, T-shirt, screen saver, or custom-made bumper sticker.

Why would you prefer to live—in a city, town, cave, jungle, or desert?

Name one similarity and one difference between you and each of us.

When did you claim you did *not* feel something when you actually did feel it (e.g. "I'm not hungry!" or "I'm not tired!")? What's the reason you did that?

Which circus job fits your personality: juggler, lion tamer, tightrope walker, clown, human cannon ball, contortionist, or knife thrower?

Repair rehearsal

Each family member identifies a time when someone hurt their feelings. What helped them recover? Did they share how they felt when it happened? Did the other person apologize, get defensive, or remain unaware of the hurt they caused? Have one family member act the role of someone whose feelings are hurt, and another family member act the role of someone making a repair. As the hurt person, share what makes it easier to forgive. As the person apologizing, share how it feels to admit to hurting someone, take responsibility, and make up.

What meal could you eat for a month straight, and why wouldn't you get sick of it?

Name your least favorite chore. What would make doing it more fun?

Which of your five senses (taste, hearing, sight, smell, touch) is sharpest or most sensitive? How does that affect you?

What was the best dream you ever had? What made it great?

Rethinking chores

Once you're clear on your least favorite chore, take turns telling your family what's going through your head when you do this chore. For example, if it's loading the dishwasher, here are the kinds of thoughts you might share: *Scraping food off plates is so gross and boring*; *I want to get this over with as soon as possible.* Next, come up with new thoughts you could think instead to change your view of this chore, such as *This is one of the ways I contribute to my family*; *It's nice to be needed*; *I like helping people.* Once everyone has tried this activity, discuss whether this changed the way it felt to do the chore.

Describe your favorite superhero's bedtime routine.

If we created a family coat of arms, what symbols would you choose to represent us?

Have you ever feared a good feeling or enjoyed a bad feeling?

If you created a tortilla chip flavor, what would it be and why would it be popular?

Superhero bedtime

Choose a part of your favorite superhero's bedtime routine that you'd like to incorporate into your existing bedtime routine. Use string or tape to turn a towel into a cape and put it on. If your superhero doesn't wear a cape, put something else on that will help you feel like them. Go to bed at your usual time, in your usual way, but include your new, adjusted superhero bedtime activity. In the morning, debrief about how you slept.

Who's been your kindest teacher so far, and what makes them special?

What's one bad habit you want to replace with a better habit? What could the better, replacement habit be?

What makes you feel better when you're lying in bed sick?

Describe your ideal home and its best feature.

Tackling transitions

If you avoid a transition, postpone it, or get irritable when it's happening, then it's probably a challenge for you. A tough transition might be getting out of bed in the morning or getting into bed at night. It might be transitioning from being at school or work to being at home. Briefly discuss challenging transitions until everyone has identified one they struggle with. What makes this transition hard for you? What would make it easier? If it's hard to wake up in the morning, could you go to bed earlier? Would a special breakfast give you the motivation you need to get going? What about playing soothing music at night to help you feel relaxed? Brainstorm ideas for each family member's tough transition, then test them out.

What's the best thing and the worst thing about being your age?

Is it easier to listen to other people share things, or to share things yourself? Why?

How do you feel when we don't notice something helpful you've done? Would you ever ask us to recognize your helpfulness?

What does your dream bedroom look like?

Wisdom from the past or future

Take turns pretending you're either ten years older or ten years younger than you are right now. How do you feel about the "worst" part of being your current age from that imaginary vantage point?

What's one of your happiest memories from when you were younger?

Is there a person or animal whose mind you wish you could read? Give us a sample of what their thoughts sound like. For extra credit, move like the animal while you do this.

When you're angry, do you hold it in or show it? How does your anger usually come out?

Describe how you envision yourself feeling, being, or acting differently next year.

What's the best part of going on your favorite playground or amusement park ride?

Tell us about a task you postponed that you wish now you'd done—and why you wish you'd done it.

How do you handle the feeling that's most difficult for you to feel?

What do you look forward to most about getting older?

What's one thing you like about us going through this journal together?

What's one thing you could do to be more responsible: go to bed on time, share toys, get outside more, drink more water and eat more vegetables, offer assistance to others in need, finish projects, keep promises, or show people more consideration and respect?

Are there situations where it's hurtful to others when you express happiness or joy?

What do you imagine missing in a few years about being the age you are now?

What would you do to make a boring place (like a doctor's office) more fun?

What do grandparents give you that's different from what parents give you?

What's the difference between when people laugh with you and when they laugh at you?

What are you scared to do, but want to do anyway?

What do you like most about having a best friend?

When you make a mistake, do you tell yourself, "I'm upset, but we all make mistakes," or "This is terrible, what's wrong with me?" How does that affect you?

How do you know when you're nervous? Do your thoughts race and your muscles get tight? Does your heart beat faster? Do you get very focused on one thing?

If we had a family awards ceremony, what's the award each of us would win?

Describe what would happen on the best day of your life.

Think of someone you judge because they have what you want. What happens to your judgment when you imagine having what they have?

When you're afraid someone will hurt your feelings, how do you protect yourself?

What would make a family weekend together extra fun (going on a picnic, doing an escape room, going to the theater, attending a sporting event, watching a movie, building a terrarium)?

Do you prefer making rules, or following them? Why?

What do the items of clothing you like to wear most say about you?

How does it feel to walk into your own home or bedroom after a long vacation?

Imagine you have the power to organize your school or work calendar. How many days off and vacation days do you have? What are your school or work hours?

On a new national holiday called Opposite Day, what would you do that's the opposite of what you normally like to do to relax?

Pick one piece of clothing you're wearing now and share a story about it.

If sadness were a thing you could magnify under a microscope, describe what you'd see.

Which book or movie character would you hang out with for a weekend and why?

Testing out opposite day

For five minutes, do the opposite—safely, and with everyone's cooperation—of what you usually do. If you'd normally sit quietly, make noise and jump up and down. If you'd normally eat with a spoon, eat with a fork. If you'd normally put shoes on your feet, put them on your head.

If you could be amazing at one sport you don't play, which one would you pick and why?

Which activities do you consider girlish, and which do you consider boyish? Where did you learn to consider these things girlish or boyish?

When someone you depend on gets sick, do you feel annoyed, scared, sad, or something else? What fears and needs go with those emotions?

A genie pops out of a bottle and grants you a wish—for another person. Who in our family would get the wish, and what would you wish for them?

What's your prize possession and under what circumstances would you give it away?

On a scale from one to five (with one being "not at all" and five being "very"), how good are you at asking for help? Why is asking for help easy or hard?

Would you want to always be happy? What would the downside be?

If you were the size of a ladybug, what hidden space in our home would you explore and what do you think you might find there?

Describe one unforgettable experience you had in nature.

What's something special about you most people don't notice?

On a scale from one to five (with one being "bad" and five being "great"), how good are you at waiting your turn for things you want?

If you built a new vehicle that defied the rules of gravity, what would it be and what purpose would it serve?

If you could only choose one form of entertainment for a party, would it be a performing clown, magician, karaoke DJ, face painter, or laser tag MC? Why would this be the best choice?

What's a thought that helps you accept tough situations you can't change?

Would filming and posting a family dance on social media make you cringe or proud?

Name your top survival skill, and say how it would save us in the wild.

Describe the stick-figure car decals you'd choose to decorate our car and represent our family.

When you feel anxious, do you reach out to people or avoid them?

When you disagree with someone, do you keep arguing with that person in your head even when they're not around? Does that calm you down or make you angrier?

What would you go back in time and change, and how might that affect the world today?

What's your favorite hobby and why do you enjoy it?

In what ways are you both like and unlike other people you've met?

On a scale from one to five (with one being "a little" and five being "a lot"), how much input do you think you have in family decisions? Give examples.

If you joined a band that makes music with kitchen items, what "instrument" would you play and why?

Kitchen band

Gather everyone together in the kitchen, at a time when you don't have to worry about disturbing neighbors. Look for items that could double as musical instruments, such as wooden serving spoons, large pots, and cutlery. Pour dry beans into a glass jar, twist on a lid, and shake it to create a maraca, or use a strip of parchment paper that crinkles loudly when you wave it. Older kids or adults may want to fill several glasses with different levels of water, and then circle their rims with a wet fingertip. Tap them (lightly!) with wooden spoons. Record a few minutes of your kitchen band music and share it with others.

What's a good thing about doing family group hugs, and how often should we do them?

In what ways is our family both like and unlike other families we know?

What's one upcoming family decision you'd like to have more input in?

What's the best way you know of to spread love and hope through the world?

Family crowdsourcing

Everyone sits in a circle, and one person summarizes a decision that's pending (such as, "Where we'll go on vacation.") Each family member offers their ideas, popcorn style (i.e. "Disney World," "We travel through Europe," "We go glamping.") Go around the circle several times, allowing everyone to share their ideas, however impractical. Close by expressing gratitude for the process of sharing ideas, whatever shape the ultimate decision takes.

What's your best quality as a friend?

What's a kind thing someone did for you recently that cheered you up?

What's an example of a situation that makes time speed up or slow down?

Ten years from now, what will you miss the most about our family life that you take for granted now?

Make up a couplet (two lines that rhyme) about something you love (e.g. "Our puppy's so sweet and cute / Her bark sounds like a broken flute").

When you really want something, what thoughts go through your head? Do your thoughts make the feeling of wanting something stronger or weaker?

In your experience, what's the difference between nervousness and excitement?

What homemade costume would win you first place at a costume party?

How could we enjoy your least favorite holiday more?

What would be good and bad about always getting your way?

What's something you secretly enjoy about being sick?

Which of the world's biggest problems would you like to get rid of and how?

Imagine all screens and the internet vanished overnight. How would you spend your free time?

What's a thought you notice going through your head right now?

What place in our home do you like that you used to dislike? What changed?

Where would you like to stop on a cross-country family road trip and what would our final destination be?

What are some pros and cons of bathing versus showering (or showering versus bathing)?

When someone hurts your feelings, what helps you forgive them? Do you need them to apologize with the right words, *do* something that shows they're sorry, or both?

What ordinary, harmless thing—for example Swiss cheese or hairballs—gives you the heebie-jeebies? Tell the story (true or made up) about why this is.

If you created a time capsule that would be opened in 150 years, what would you put in it for your great, great-grandchildren's entertainment?

Family time capsule

Find an empty shoe box. Give everyone five minutes to find one or two small, nonessential items that represent something important to them. Place these items in the box. If you prefer, write a note to your future self rather than selecting items. Include what you like about your life right now, what you think about, how you feel about your friends and others who have an impact on you, and what your biggest dream is.

After everyone puts their items or notes inside the box, tape the lid shut, date it, and put it in a drawer or closet. Write a reminder on a calendar. If you prefer, set a digital reminder for whatever length of time you like (a month, six months, or even a year). When the preset time arrives, reopen the box. Take your time rediscovering the items or papers you placed within it. Share your thoughts with each other about what's changed in the time period that's passed.

If you had to play a musical instrument (or a different one from the instrument you already play), which one would you pick and why?

What's a mean thing you secretly say to yourself that you'd like to stop saying?

What's something that makes you feel small when you look at it (but in a good way)—for example clouds, stars, or the ocean? Describe that feeling in detail.

Create a meaningful custom license plate for your dream car between eight and ten letters or numbers long and explain its meaning.

If you could effortlessly acquire a skill or talent, what would it be?

Why do you think our brains say mean things to us?

What feels different about running into someone you like versus running into someone you don't care about much?

Imagine past lives are real. What animal were you before and how does that animal show up in your behavior now?

Inner meanie networking event

Recall some of the mean things you secretly say to yourselves, and allow yourselves to embody your inner meanies. Take on their postures and facial expressions. Change your hair, wear your glasses upside down. Allow yourself to walk around the room the way your inner meanies would walk, stomp, or crawl. Sit the way they'd sit; stand the way they'd stand. Take on all their inner meanie mannerisms.

Once everyone feels like they've captured the spirit of their inner meanies, give your meanies a name. Have them introduce themselves to each other and shake hands or exchange high-fives. Then, have them explain why they're so mean to you (their hosts) and what they hope to accomplish by saying mean things to you. Finally, thank them for showing up, and tell them you appreciate how they're trying to help you, and invite them to let you handle things differently—without meanness—in the future.

What's something you saw while traveling that you never saw at home?

What tough situation did someone handle poorly? How would you handle it better?

What part of being kind to people feels good?

Imagine sending a friend or family member a care package. What's in it?

____

____

____

____

____

Random act of gifting

Spend a few minutes over the course of the next week gathering a few small, inexpensive, meaningful items you'd like to send someone you care about. Write your gift box recipient a short note—and don't be afraid to tell them how you hope the items in the box will brighten their day. With the help of a parent or older sibling if you need it, prepare your gift box and send it. Let yourself experience the pleasure that comes from being thoughtful and generous.

If you had a time machine, where would you go, and what would you do there?

What tough situation did someone handle well? Would you handle it the same way?

What part of being unkind feels bad?

What's one wish you'd make right now on a shooting star?

Describe the strangest object in your room in detail without using its name. We each get one shot at guessing what it is.

____

____

____

____

____

Where do you think your body's main control center is located—your head, gut, heart, or some other place? Why?

____

____

____

____

____

How does it feel when you think imagine what life was like on earth before humans?

____

____

____

____

____

Describe what would be a great sleepover or vacation with a few friends.

Shooting star wishes

Go somewhere outside together when the sky is dark and cloudless. Point out stars you see and talk about them. Can you guess how many light-years away they are? How big are they? Are they real stars, planets, or satellites? Look for a shooting star. If you see one, make a wish. If you don't see one, make a wish on an imaginary shooting star. Both types of wishes are equally likely to come true.

What do you like most about being around people outside our family?

What do you imagine your first thought was when you were born?

Describe a recent situation that made you laugh.

What family tradition have you outgrown? What's a new one you'd replace it with?

What's one thing you like about being alone?

What's good about making mistakes, and what's bad about being perfect?

Describe a few thoughts and sensations that go with jealousy.

Describe what you'd want us to bring on our ideal family picnic.

Give an example of a time you got motivated to do something boring—and ended up enjoying yourself.

What's the thought you have most often when you open your eyes in the morning?

What's the difference between how you feel with friends and how you feel with us?

Describe a dream you had recently that felt so real you thought you were awake.

Family dream journaling

Write down your dreams for a week. Every night, remind one another that you'll be journaling about dreams as a family. Keep several pens, a small notebook, and a flashlight by your bed. For those of you who wake up once or twice in the middle of the night to go to the bathroom, jot down a few words or phrases when you do. For those who sleep through the night, the minute you wake up, jot down what you were dreaming about immediately, before getting out of bed. When the week is over, sit down together, review what you wrote, and share the dreams that stood out. Notice if there are any similarities between the people, plots, themes, or places you dreamed about.

What made the best gift you ever received special?

Walk us through how one small thought could affect the rest of your day.

What do you feel most at school or work, and how does that affect your actions?

What's a small step you're able to take right now toward one of your biggest goals?

How-small-can-you-go game

Identify a goal that's big for you. Maybe it's making a new friend, building a spaceship in your backyard, getting physically stronger, or saving up money for something you want. Draw your goal—or write it down—at the top of a piece of paper. Now share your papers with one another. Write down a small step that the person who wrote it could take toward reaching their goal. Continue passing these goals around and writing down smaller and smaller steps until you can't think of any more. Each family member keeps the paper with their big goal at the top and the list of small-step suggestions beneath it.

Out of all modes of transportation, which do you like most and why?

What are some pros and cons of looking at things on screens a lot?

PROMPTS

When you feel shame, would telling someone you trust, "I feel ashamed right now," make the feeling grow or fade away?

What are you excited about that's happening in the next month?

How would you repaint the outside of our home to get us on the local news?

If your brain had only five compartments for things you think about (such as family, friends, toys, sports, food, books, school, music, or games), what would yours be?

What's the scariest thing that ever happened to you and how did you handle it?

Create a sculpture out of any small items you see around you right now and explain its meaning.

What's the most fascinating object you found on a beach?

What's something you thought you couldn't do, then surprised yourself by doing well?

What's something you saw or heard today that made you smile?

How do you most want others to see you (as kind, strong, smart, funny, stylish, creative, or athletic), and what new habit would help you become more like that?

What do you enjoy doing as a family that we haven't done for a while?

Name a few things you've noticed people do when they're trying to get attention. What do you do when you're trying to get attention?

Name one thing you wanted to get done today but didn't. Do you feel regretful thinking about it, or energized to do it tomorrow?

What would be fun about adopting one of your friends as a permanent member of our family?

A week of family fun

Put a calendar on a wall (make one if you don't have one). Review what different family members identified as the thing they enjoy doing most as a family. If necessary, adjust the activities your family members mentioned in ways that make them more doable. If the activities require travel, come up with a version of the activity that fits your family's schedule. How many of these activities fit into one week?

What's the coolest thing about the coolest car you've ever seen?

Share what you learned from a time when a friend hurt your feelings.

What purpose does feeling guilt serve?

If you created a dream team out of a few of today's top athletes, who'd be on it and what would the team be called?

What's the most fun you've had staying up late?

Imagine you had to hide in a room without technology for 24 hours. What would you do to entertain yourself?

When did you have a gut feeling you were glad you followed?

What cause would you want to raise money for or donate time to, and why would it be worth it to make that sacrifice?

The silent treatment

Choose a time where you're usually talkative—such as during a meal, taking a walk, or playing a game. Set a timer for 15 minutes and use only gestures, facial expressions, and eye contact to communicate. Afterward, discuss how it felt to remain silent. Did you feel connected to yourself and others? Did you notice things you don't notice when you're busy talking or thinking about what to say? Did the time go by quickly or slowly?

How would you sum up your favorite movie in five words or fewer?

What's a situation where being kind was more important than being right?

How do we respond to people getting angry in our family? How could we handle anger better?

What famous group of real or imaginary people would you like our family to dress up as someday?

What would you enjoy most about riding in a fire truck, police car, dump truck, horse and buggy, trailer bike, or ambulance?

What's a situation where speaking your mind was more important than being liked?

When you feel proud, how do you show it? How could we help you show it more?

If we created a secret family handshake, what would it be? Show us.

Brag-a-thon

Every family member thinks of something they did today that they're proud of, or that made them feel happy. Examples of bragworthy actions are: "I put my dish in the sink after dinner"; "I went for a long walk and enjoyed nature"; "I told a joke and made a friend laugh hard"; and "My art teacher hung my painting on a wall." No matter what the bragging person says, other family members celebrate them by clapping, cheering, or saying, "That's great! You should be proud of that. I'm proud of you, too." Share with each other how it feels to express pride in yourself, and to hear others celebrate what you shared, and feel proud of you, too.

What's the silliest thing you did with a friend?

What do most adults get wrong about kids?

When you feel loving, how do you show it? How could we help you show it more?

What do you think people's dreams and goals reveal about their personality?

Act out a short ad for your favorite food.

What do most kids get wrong about adults?

When you feel sad, how do you show it?
How could we help you show it more?

If we ever got separated in a crowd and didn't have phones, what loud or high-pitched call or cry would help us find each other again? Teach us how to make it.

Secret support signal

Everyone chooses a hand signal they want other family members to give them when they're experiencing an emotionally challenging moment. Choose something that reminds you of a small action that will help you feel calmer. One person might ask others to raise three fingers in the air to remind them to take three deep breaths. Someone who's self-critical might ask others to make a heart shape with their hands as a reminder that they're loveable. Give family members these hand signals whenever you think they need them.

Name your three best traits.

If your anger were a monster, what would it look like?

If you had the power to change one human flaw we all have, what would it be? Why do you think we'd survive longer as a species without that flaw?

____

____

____

____

____

Angry monster art

Get some paper and some colored markers or crayons. Place the paper on a table or floor and draw your anger with gusto. Whether or not you're feeling angry as you do this, connect with what anger feels like in your body. Do you feel anger in your stomach and throat? In your head and chest? See what colors fit your anger best. Reds? Blacks? Greens? What kinds of lines express its energy? Zigzags? Circles? Or lots of little lines or dots? Does your anger have a face? Does it have hands? Is your anger a force or energy—like wind or fire? When everyone has created a drawing, discuss your monsters as a family and share what you think you need to give them to help them calm down.

What do you like best about your favorite selfie or photo?

Name the three best traits of each of us here.

If you had to put on a large crown, a fake mustache, or a poop emoji hat in public, which would you choose and why?

On a cold, snowy night, what family activity would help us bond and feel cozy?

Family dress-up

Sit down as a family with paper, pens, crayons, string, and tape, and create the object you said you'd feel most confident wearing in public. When you're done, put on your creation and decide where you'll go as a family wearing your gear. Document your adventure in a video or selfie.

What do you look forward to most about a yearly event or holiday?

Has seeing another person's viewpoint in an argument ever changed your mind?

Is there a place you could go to when you feel sad that would be comforting—even if you only went there in your mind? What would comfort you about it?

What would motivate you to wear fancy clothes to bed or PJs to a fancy party?

Logically explain why you eat a certain food with your fingers that most people eat with a fork (or vice versa).

If you had to perform in front of a crowd, what would you do?

Who or what do you feel responsible for? Does that responsibility weigh you down or make you feel purposeful?

What would be the best and worst part of our family living on a tropical island?

Favorite family meal week

Create a meal schedule for the week that includes at least one of each family members' favorite meals. Take turns cooking the favorite meal of the day, or make the meals together. Include all family members in this process, no matter how old or young they are. Make meal prep easier by deciding in advance who'll go to the store and buy ingredients, who'll chop and prep, and who'll do clean-up.

What kind of jewelry do you like the best and why?

What could we do better as a family in the morning to set ourselves up for a good day?

When people say things about your character or personality that are true but hard to hear, how do you react?

Which would you want to discover most: a cure for a disease, a planet, a civilization, a dinosaur, or something else?

What's each person's favorite snack in our family?

What could we do better in the evening to set ourselves up for a peaceful night's rest?

If someone says "no" to a request you make, how would it feel to respond, "Thank you for taking care of yourself"?

Scientists say your odds of being born are one in 400 trillion. If you really understood how rare and precious you truly are, how would you live your life differently?

Gratitude touchpoint

Call to mind one thing you're grateful for about a family member once a day. When you're sitting down to a meal, traveling together, hanging out, or saying goodnight, tell them what it is about who they are (or something they've done) that you're grateful for. Ask them to use the technique of reflective listening (see 'Family Soft Skills') to demonstrate that they've heard and absorbed what you've just said.

What's the best part about someone cuddling with you before bed, wishing you a good night, or tucking you in?

Where could you have a multimillion-dollar hot chocolate or lemonade stand? What challenges would you face?

What helps you get sleepier at night when you're having trouble relaxing?

If you wrote a book, would it be poetry, self-help, a comic book, short stories, or something else? What would it be about?

If you could invent a new job, what would it be, and why would you be good at it?

If you had a robot friend who complimented you all the time, would that make it harder for you to hear criticism?

What do you do to defuse a tense conversation: make jokes, act nice, or pretend as if nothing is happening?

Explain why you think it would be more fun to go surfing, ride down a water slide, or have a family water balloon battle.

Which day of the week do you like more than the others and why?

Why, if someone bumps into you, do you say "Excuse me"—or wait for them to say it?

How do you handle disappointment, and how could you handle it better?

What wild animal (kangaroo, mouse, urban fox, python, or squirrel) gets a bad rap, and would make a good house pet?

What made you think you'd hate a food you ended up liking, and how did you end up trying it?

Who did you judge a little too harshly today? What did your judgment say about your mood or stress level?

Pick something you're feeling right now and act it out until we guess the feeling.

What nice thing do you wish people would say about you behind your back?

How could we make it easier for you to share your opinions on things?

Do you try to make stress disappear by putting things off till later, or by getting them done right away?

What was the happiest moment you ever had relaxing into someone's arms?

If you were a grandparent, what would you do with your grandkids so they talked about how much fun they have with you even when you're not around?

When do you wish we would leave you alone more, and when do you wish we'd get more involved?

How hard is it for you to transition from something fun to something less fun? What would make it easier for you?

How does stress make you feel, and what do you do when you feel that way?

If we had a family pillow fight competition, what rules would we follow to keep it fun and how would we decide who won?

Pillow fight

Pick the biggest, safest room for a pillow fight. Before beginning, make sure you're using pillows without zippers or buttons to avoid accidental injuries. Agree on pillow placement boundaries, such as no hits above the chest. Also, be sure to choose a safeword like "stop" that everyone agrees to follow. Decide on the prize for the pillow fight champion and set a time limit of one minute for each round. Then, gather your pillows, and let the games begin!

What is it about your favorite stuffed animal, blanket, or pillow that comforts or relaxes you at night?

Name an activity that makes you more aware of your body, and one that makes you less aware of it.

When you're feeling stressed, is there something you do without realizing it—like overeat, bite your nails, talk fast, or oversleep?

What silly thing would you do, such as having a snowball fight in a bathing suit, if you cared less about what other people think?

What amazing feat did a character in a movie do that you hope to do one day?

When something happens that you don't like, do you act like it didn't happen? Give an example. What happens when you do that?

What are your ideas for handling stress better?

What would be the best way to greet people if we couldn't use words?

Which one of your scars, moles, or birthmarks do you like, and why?

If you were offered a marshmallow right away, or five marshmallows in an hour, would you take one now or five later? Why?

What's the most important thing you've ever learned about your own feelings?

What hard thing have you done that didn't seem worth it, but was?

Chore trade

Go over each family members' chores. What does everyone do to contribute to keeping your home running smoothly? Chores include setting the table, clearing the table, washing dishes, loading the dishwasher, properly disposing of garbage, recycling, or compost, doing laundry, folding laundry, vacuuming rugs, feeding and taking pets on walks, and cleaning out the fridge. If a child in your family still hasn't taken on a chore, have everyone else in the family share with them how doing chores helped them and what it feels like to contribute to the family. Ask them if they're ready to take on a chore. If they are, let them choose a chore they'd like to be responsible for. Finally, decide on which chores you'll be trading with another family member for just one day. Once the chore trade is accomplished and completed, debrief about the experience.

What are the best things about your favorite season?

Which is harder: admitting to a mistake or defending yourself against a false accusation?

When have you acted unhappier than you are and why?

What's something we've never done before that our whole family could do on New Year's Eve this year?

What's the best way we show you love (hugs, smiles, compliments, helping you with things, or small presents)?

On a spectrum where one is "very introverted," three is "introvert–extrovert mix," and five is "very extroverted," where would each person in our family fall?

When have you acted happier than you are and why?

Love days

Write down each family member's name and preferred form of affection (e.g. compliments, hugs, smiles, help, small presents) on a piece of paper. Then place or tape it someplace where everyone will see it several times a day. Show your family members affection in the way they've said they prefer each time you see the paper.

Most-wanted compliments party

Every family member writes down five compliments they'd enjoy hearing most. These compliments might include things like: *you're so smart, you're a caring person, you're thoughtful and kind, you have the best sense of humor, you're an amazing cook, you help so much around the house, you're a loving parent*, or *you're the best child a parent could ever wish for.* Have each family member take turns sitting in a chair in the middle of the room. Whoever is seated in the chair remains still while all other family members circle them, enthusiastically saying their most-wanted compliments out loud.

Conclusion

You did it! You've tackled over 300 prompts as a family, and you've engaged in all kinds of creative activities together. You've practiced tuning in to your body, being open and receptive, listening deeply, sharing honestly, showing consideration, expressing encouragement, and resolving conflicts. Most importantly, you've maintained enough flexibility in your schedules and mindsets to convene regularly as a family and spend quality time together.

During that time, you've accomplished a lot. You've developed feeling literacy. You've spent less energy trying to convince others to like what you like and think how you think and more energy being curious about them. You've practiced metacognition skills, engaged in self-reflection, and done your best to receive feedback gracefully.

You've had moments when your suspicions about family members' preferences, thoughts, feelings, hopes and dreams were confirmed—and moments when you learned something new. You've become more thoughtful, and you've dreamed big dreams together. You've increased your collective resilience and antifragility. Chances are, there's been a lot of growth in your family ecosystem.

If you completed the Family Connection Assessment before starting your journey (or halfway through), consider retaking it now. It might be fun and informative to share what you think your closing assessment scores reveal about how far you've come. Have your scores shifted in some areas and not in others? In what way? Have you revisited the Family Soft Skills Checklist regularly and practiced specific interpersonal skills? Which ones do you think you got better at? Have you faced unexpected situations while going through this journal that led you to adjust your expectations or your approach?

Here are a few closing prompts to help you reflect on your journey together.

- What I liked most about going through this journal was ...
- What I found most challenging was ...
- A dream a family member shared that I want to support is ...
- A preference that helped me understand a family member better is ...
- What I learned about my relationship to my thoughts is ...
- Something unexpected I've learned about our family is ...
- What I learned about our family's relationship to feelings is ...
- How this experience met (or fell short of) my original intention was ...
- A new intention I have moving forward is ...
- Something we did as a family that I hope we keep doing is ...

Remember: the choose-your-own-adventure you've embarked on doesn't end when you close this book. The family experiences you've had on this journey will serve as a template for future adventures as you continue embracing what it means to be fully human in relationships.

Acknowledgments

I'm grateful to my agent, Rita Rosenkranz, who was instrumental in helping this book idea evolve into a manuscript, and to Aminatta Forna, who offered sage advice on dogs and publishing when I needed it most. Peter Noonan and Bethany Letiecq, you're both living proof that chosen family is priceless and can fall into your lap when and where you least expect it. Katherine Weider, I couldn't wish for a more expansive thinking partner and creative ally. And finally, this acknowledgments section wouldn't be complete without a shout-out to my mom, who continues showing me how to be a force of nature at every stage of life.

Your Notes

RAISING READERS

Books Build Bright Futures

Dear Reader,

We'd love your attention for one more page to tell you about the crisis in children's reading, and what we can all do.

Studies have shown that reading for fun is the **single biggest predictor of a child's future life chances** – more than family circumstance, parents' educational background or income. It improves academic results, mental health, wealth, communication skills, ambition and happiness.[1]

The number of children reading for fun is in rapid decline. Young people have a lot of competition for their time. In 2024, 1 in 10 children and young people in the UK aged 5 to 18 did not own a single book at home.[2]

Hachette works extensively with schools, libraries and literacy charities, but here are some ways we can all raise more readers:

- Reading to children for just 10 minutes a day makes a difference
- Don't give up if children aren't regular readers – there will be books for them!
- Visit bookshops and libraries to get recommendations
- Encourage them to listen to audiobooks
- Support school libraries
- Give books as gifts

There's a lot more information about how to encourage children to read on our website: **www.RaisingReaders.co.uk**

Thank you for reading.

hachette UK

[1] OECD, '21st-Century Readers: Developing Literacy Skills in a Digital World', 2021, https://www.oecd.org/en/publications/21st-century-readers_a83d84cb-en.html

[2] National Literacy Trust, 'Book Ownership in 2024', November 2024, https://literacytrust.org.uk/research-services/research-reports/book-ownership-in-2024